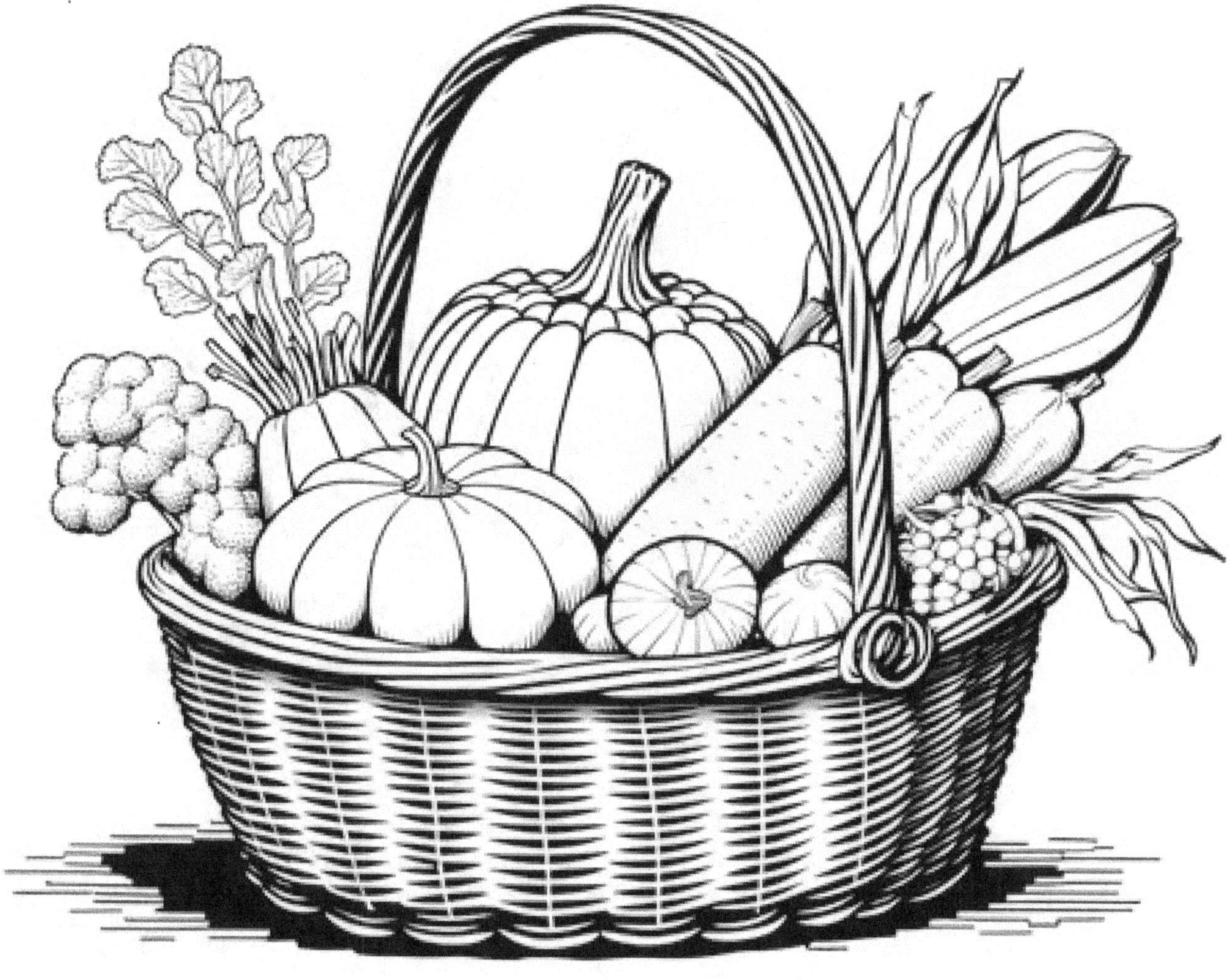

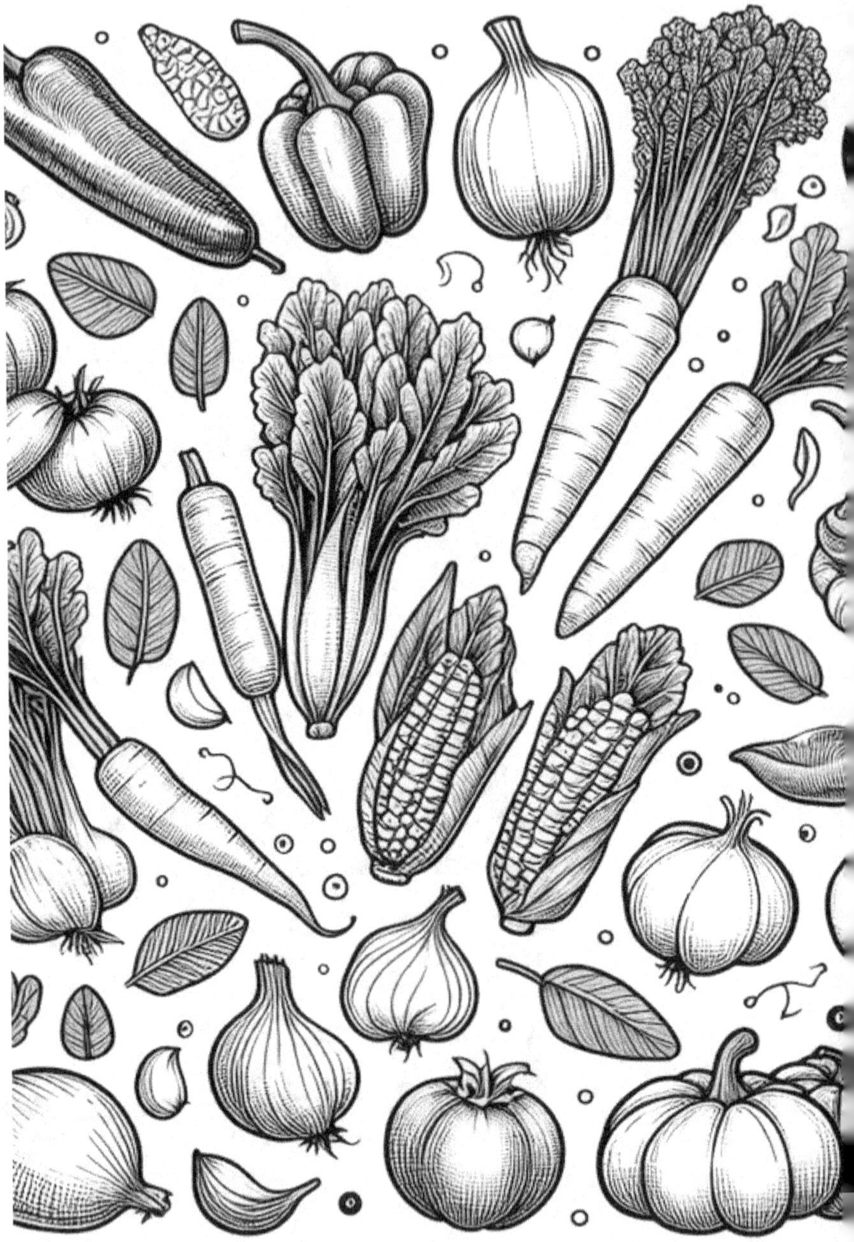

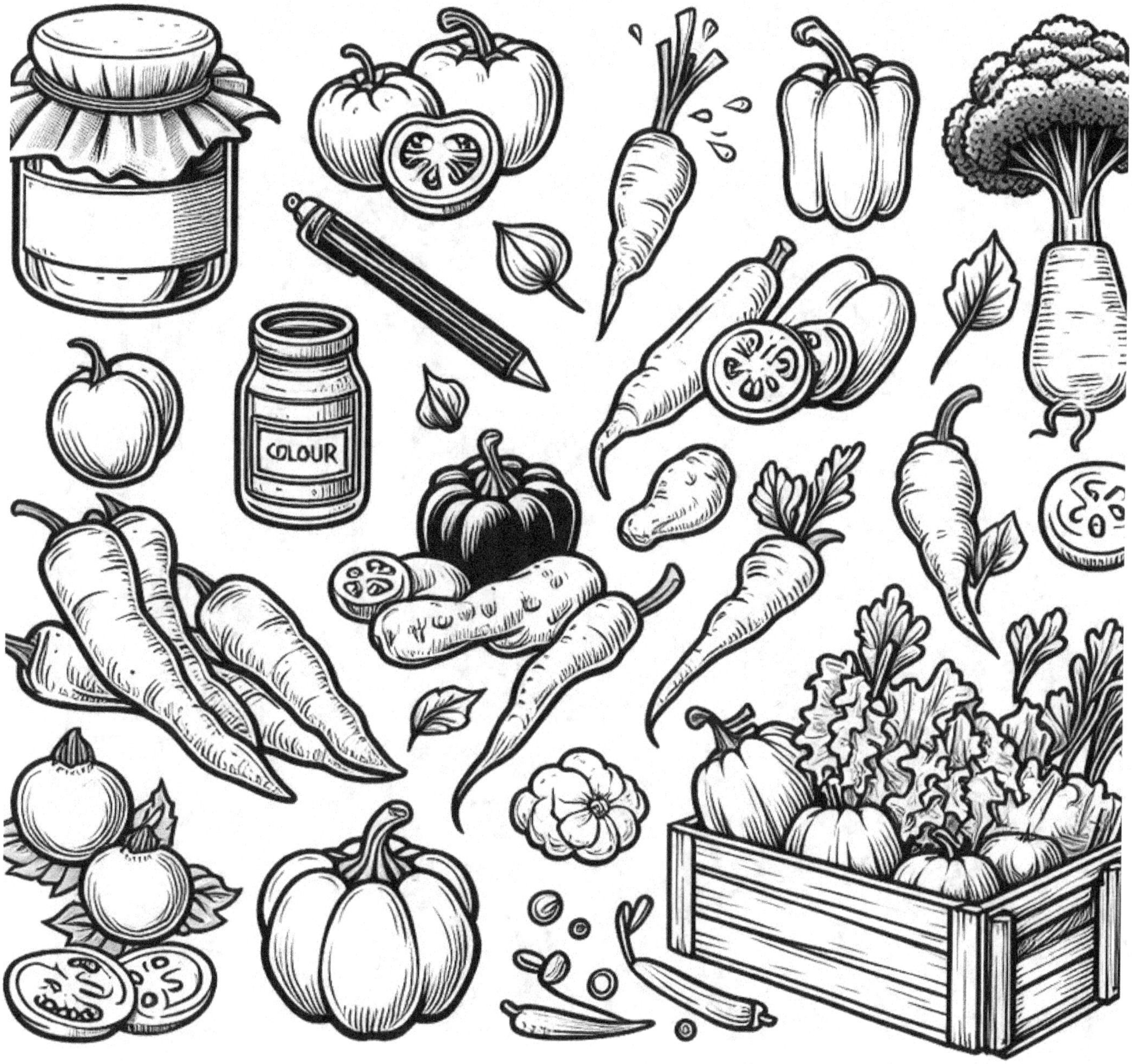
COLOUR

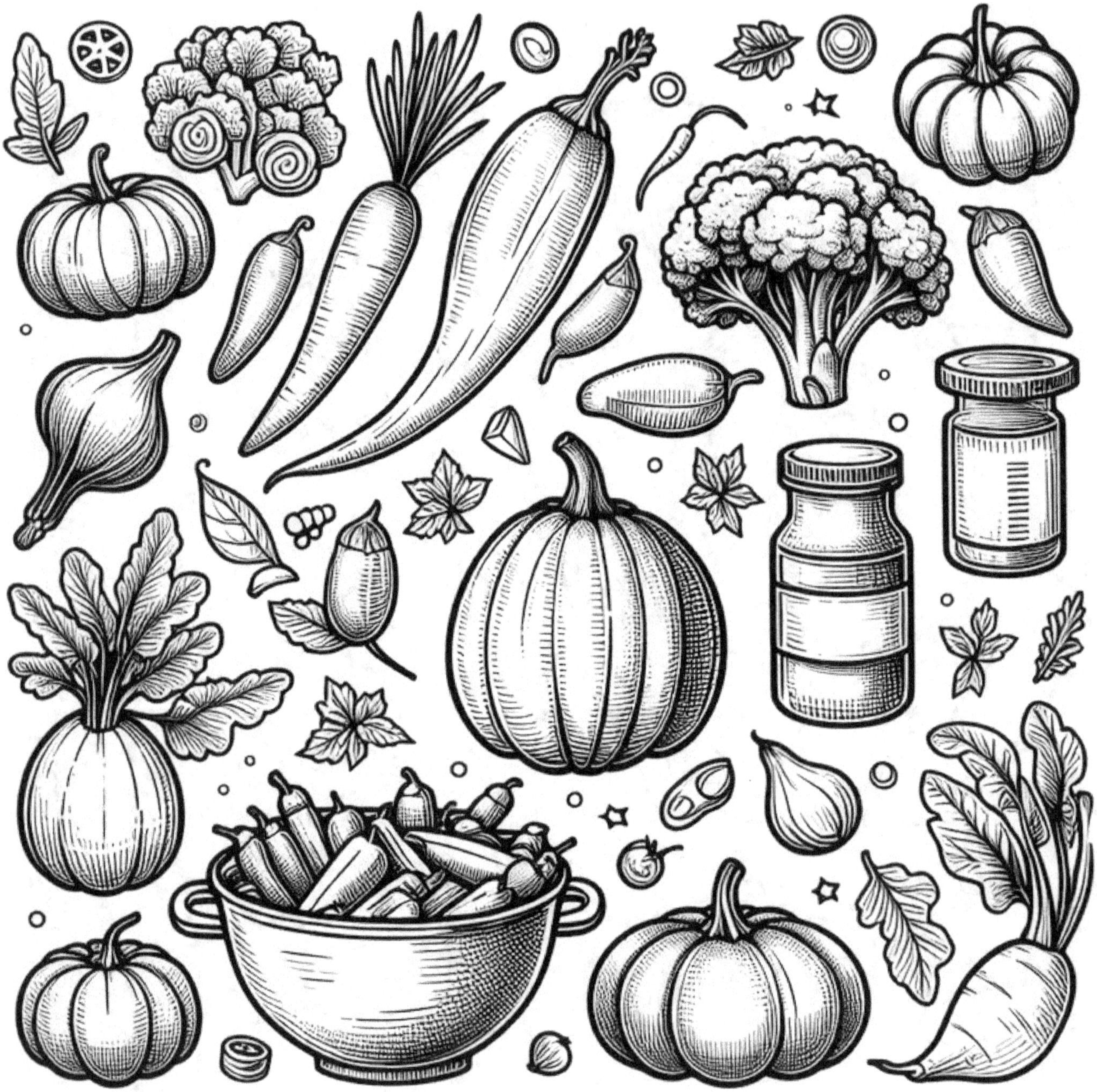

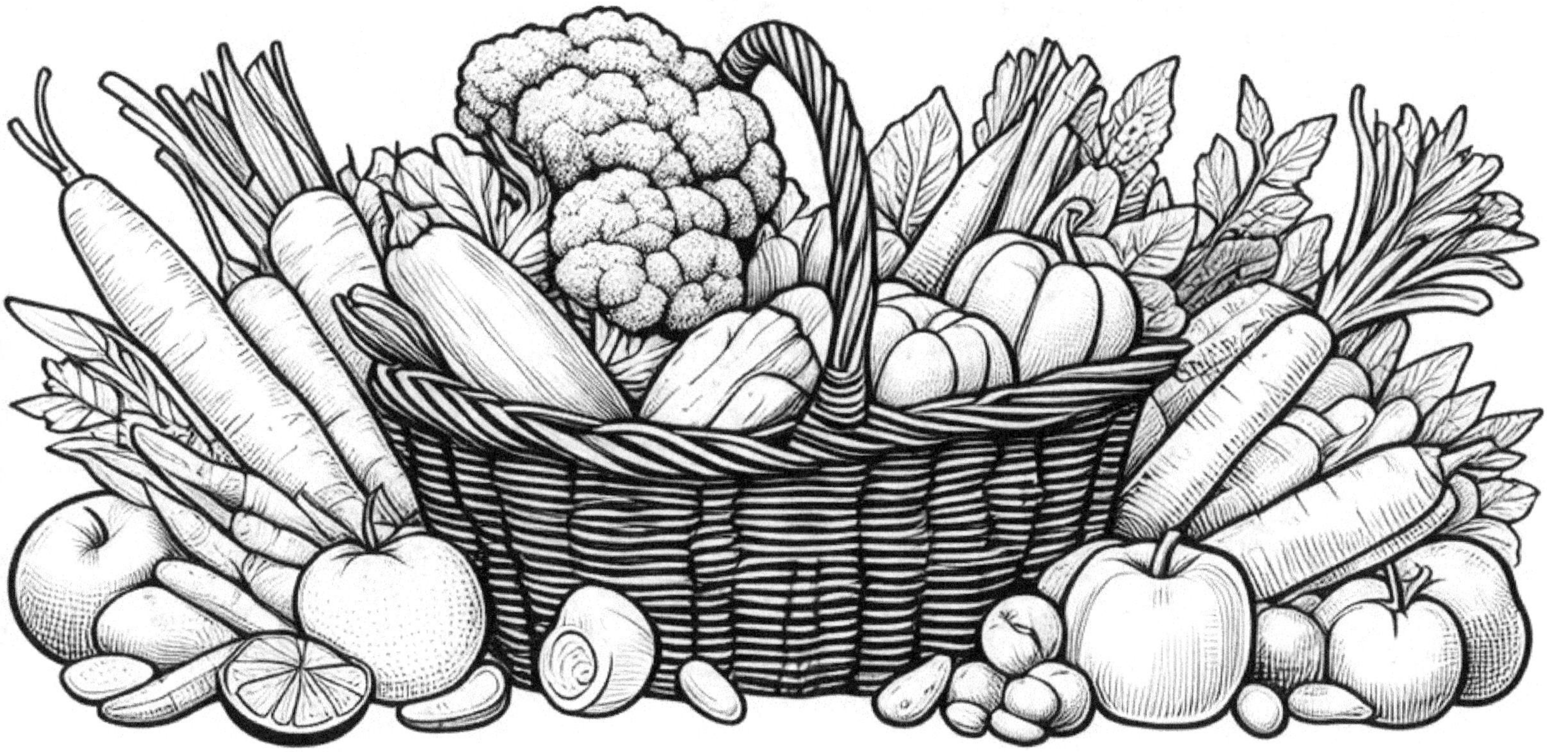

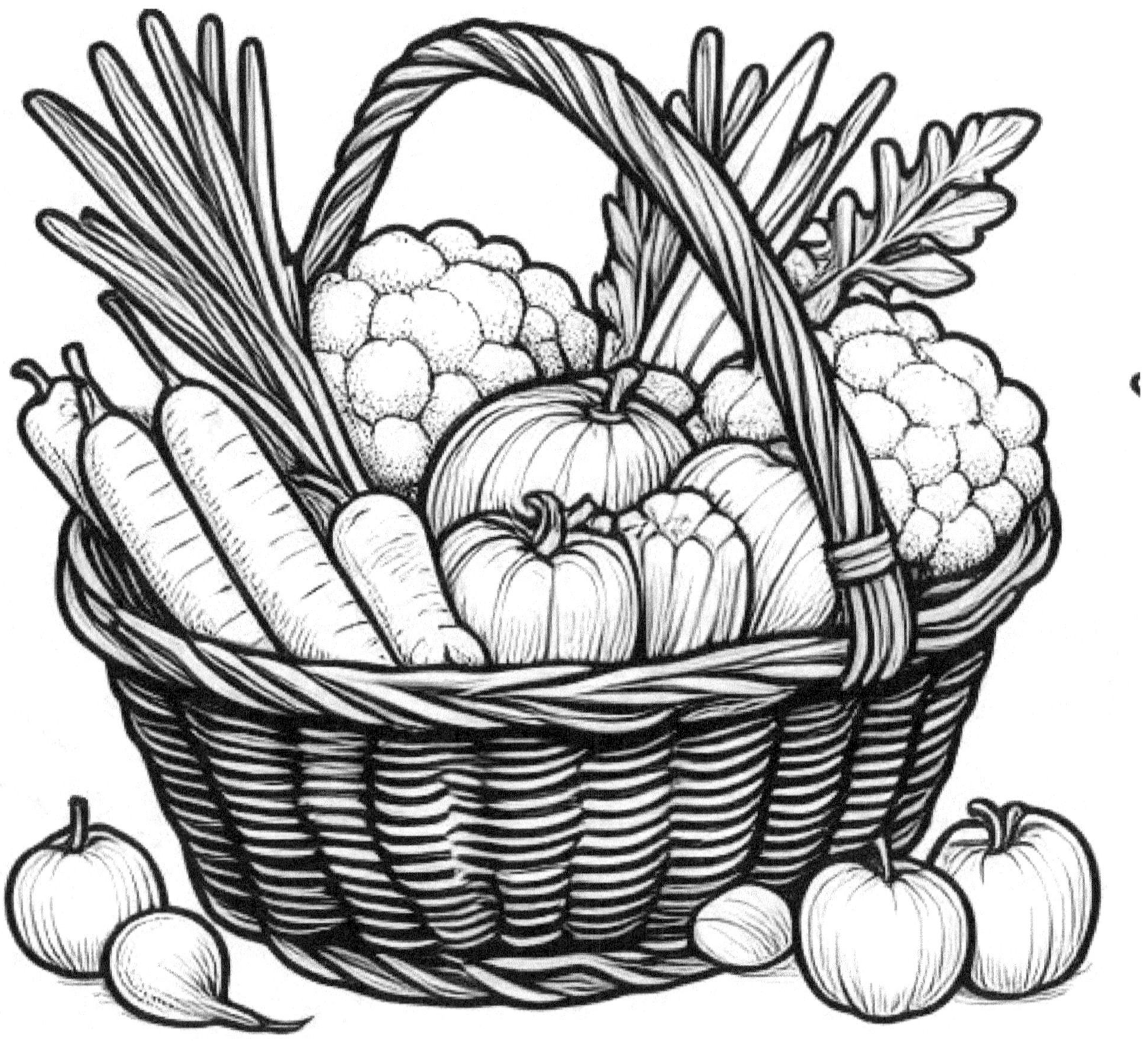

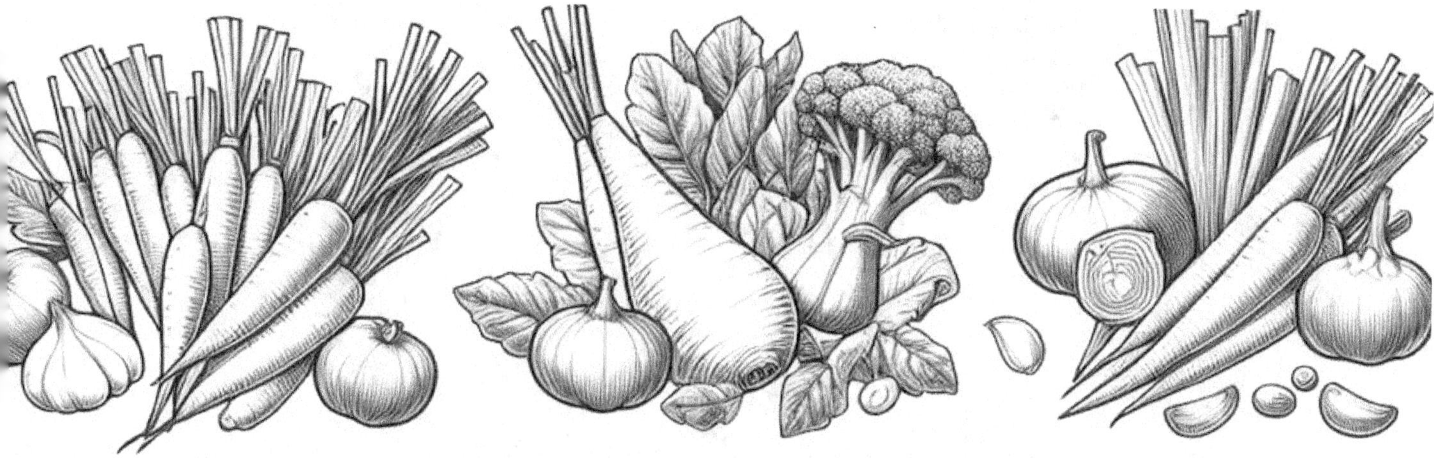

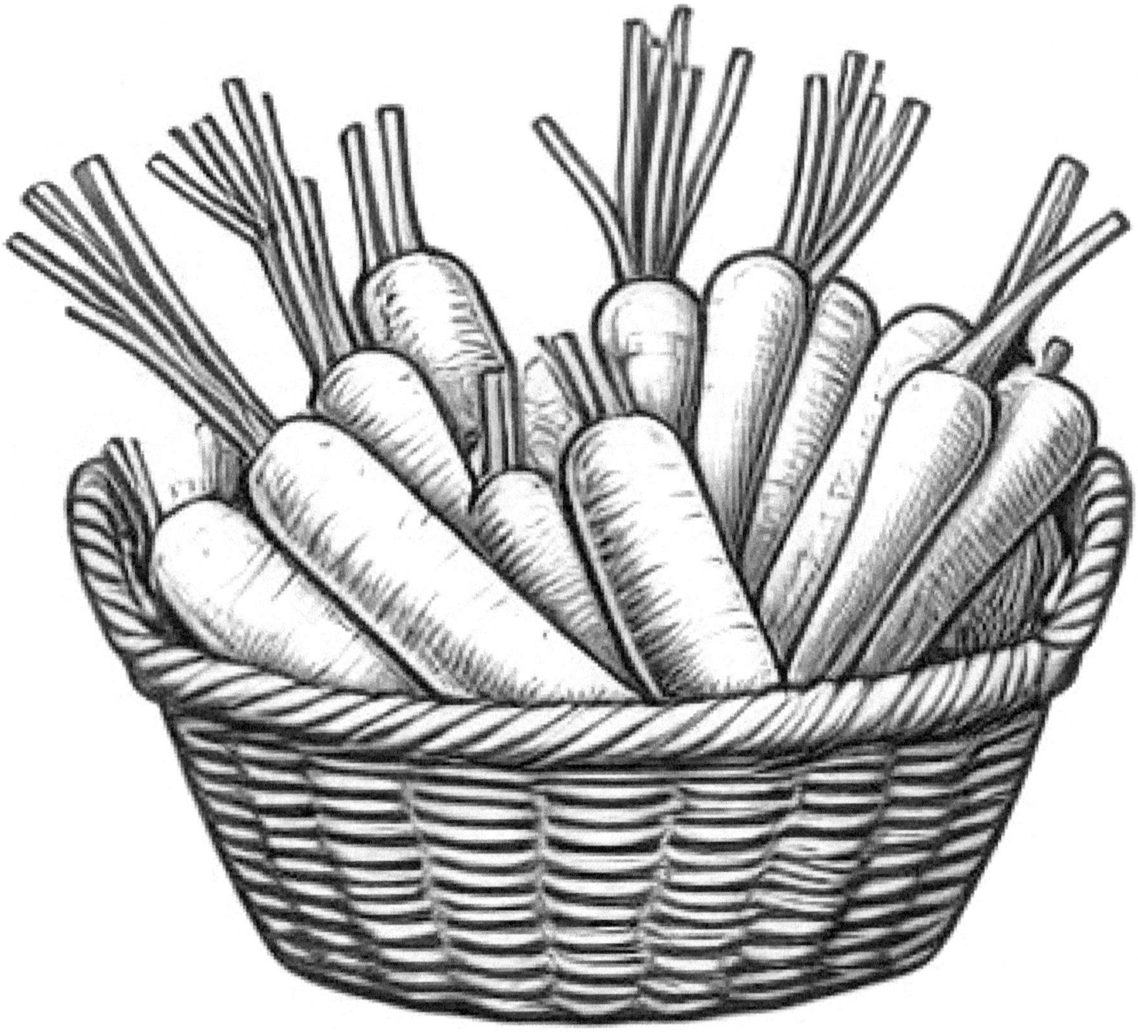

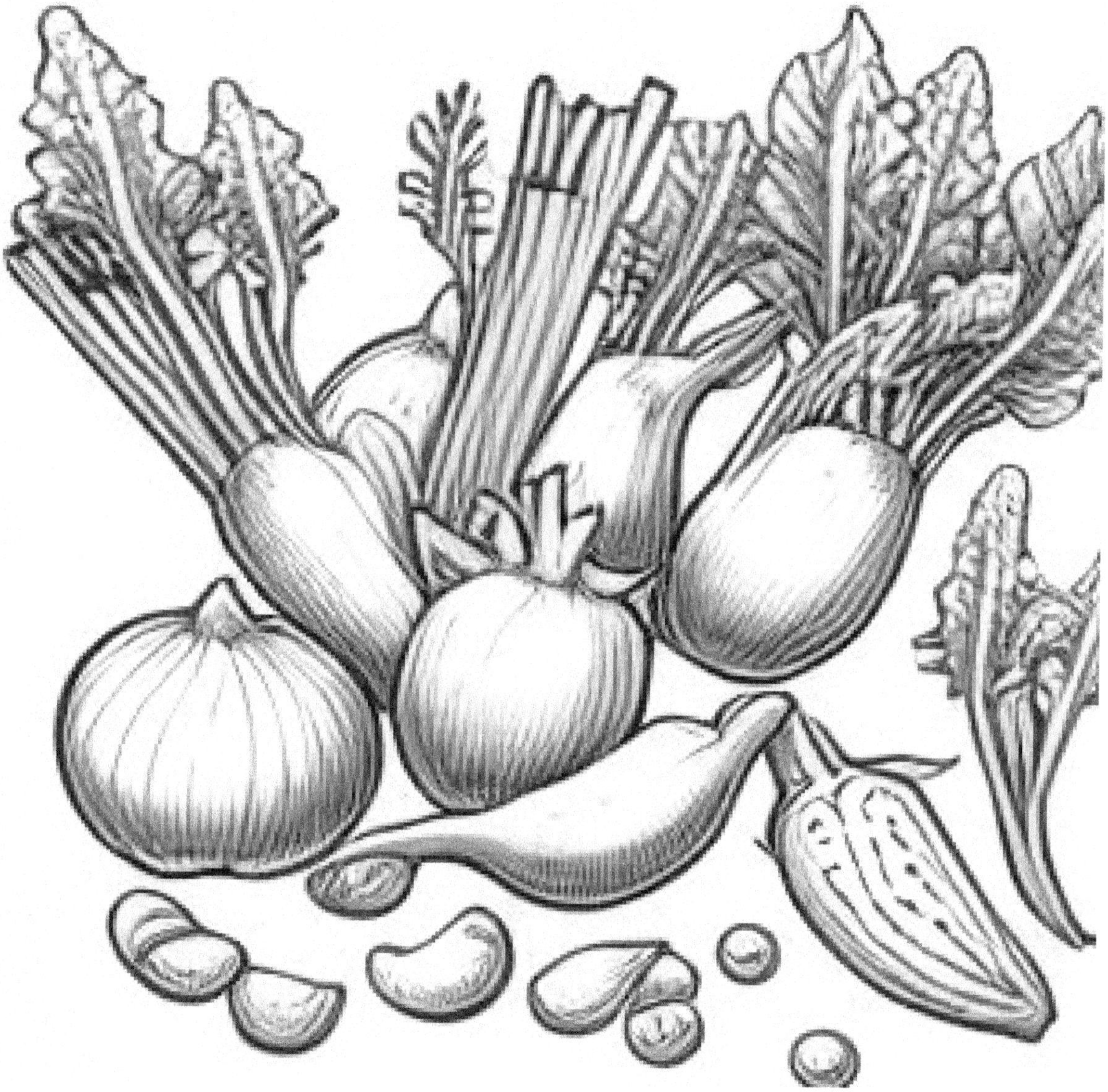

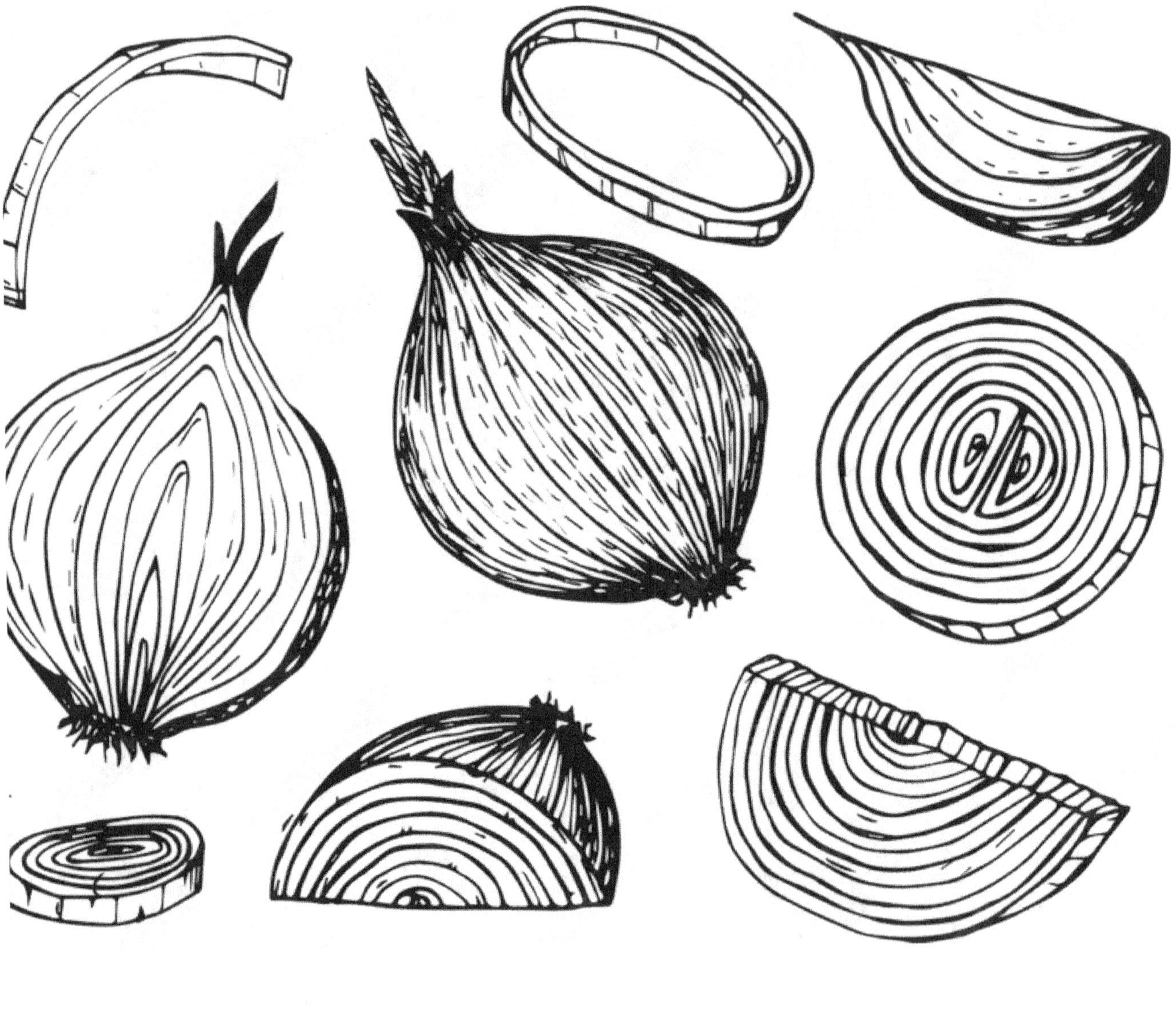

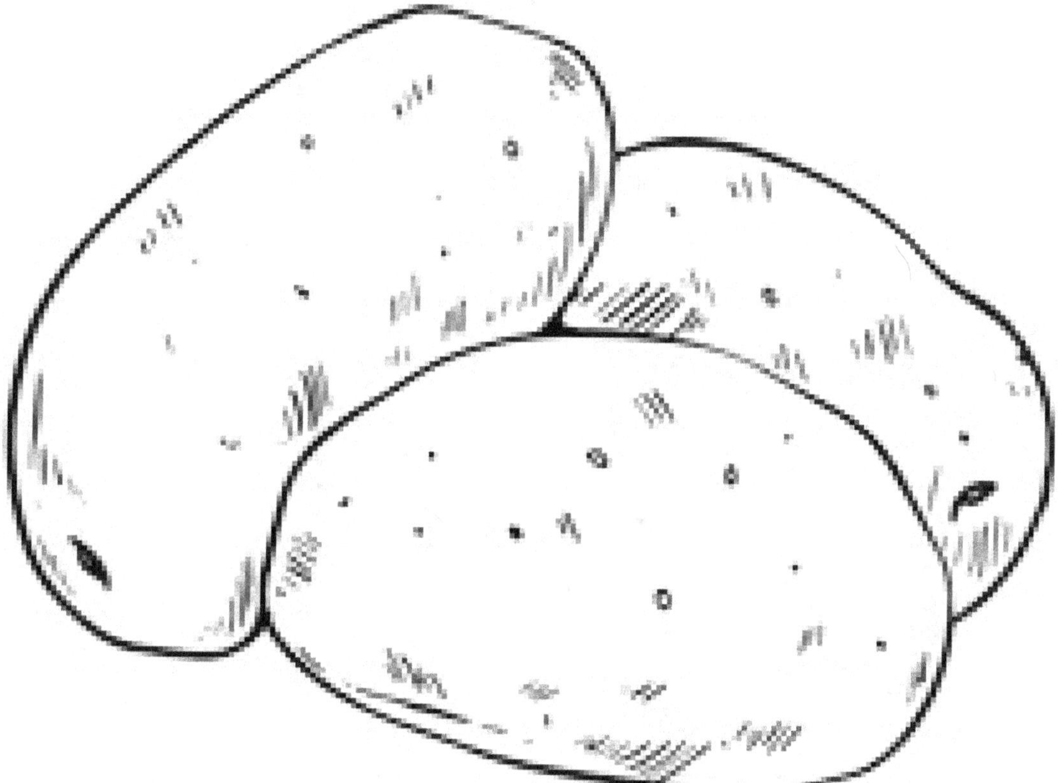

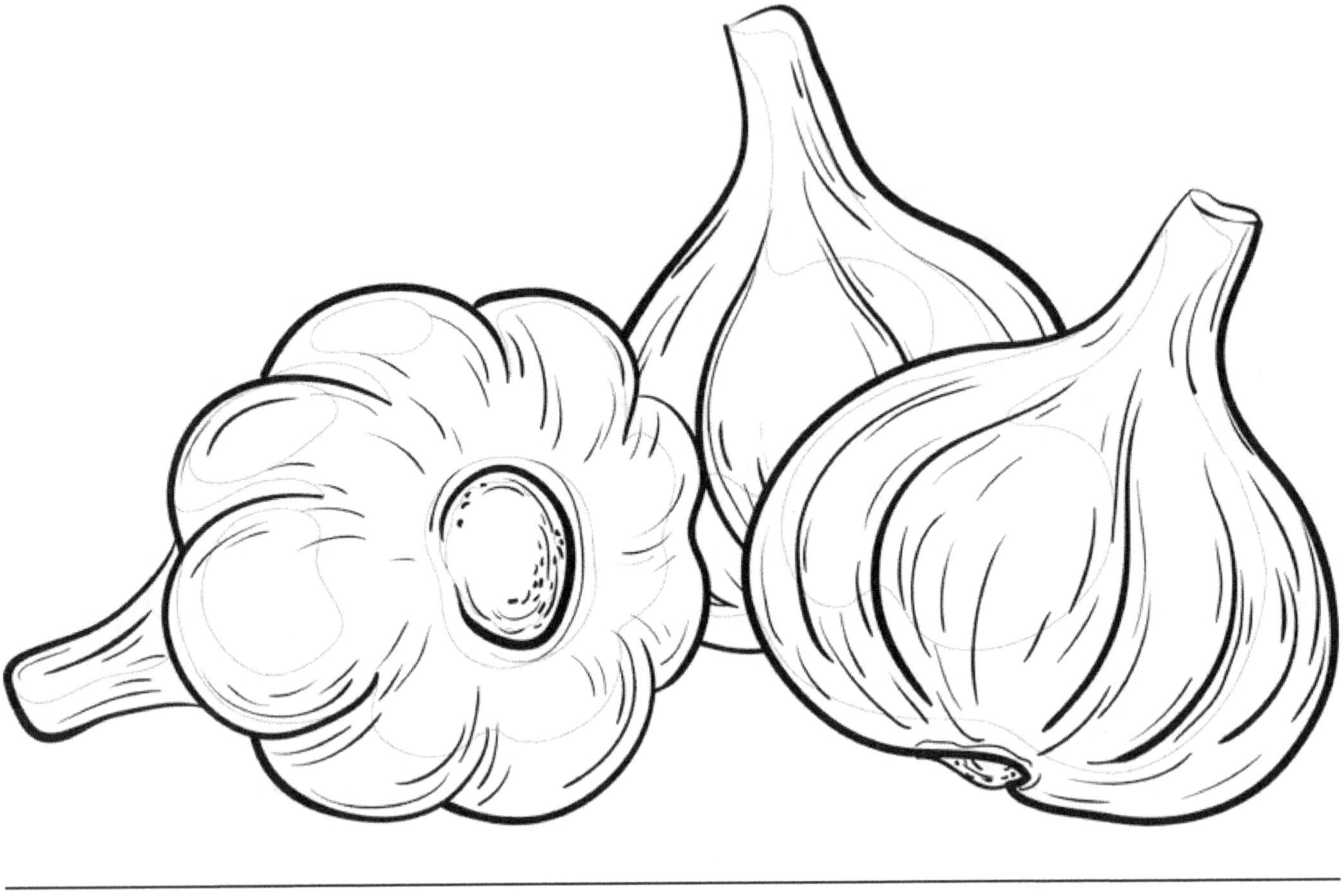

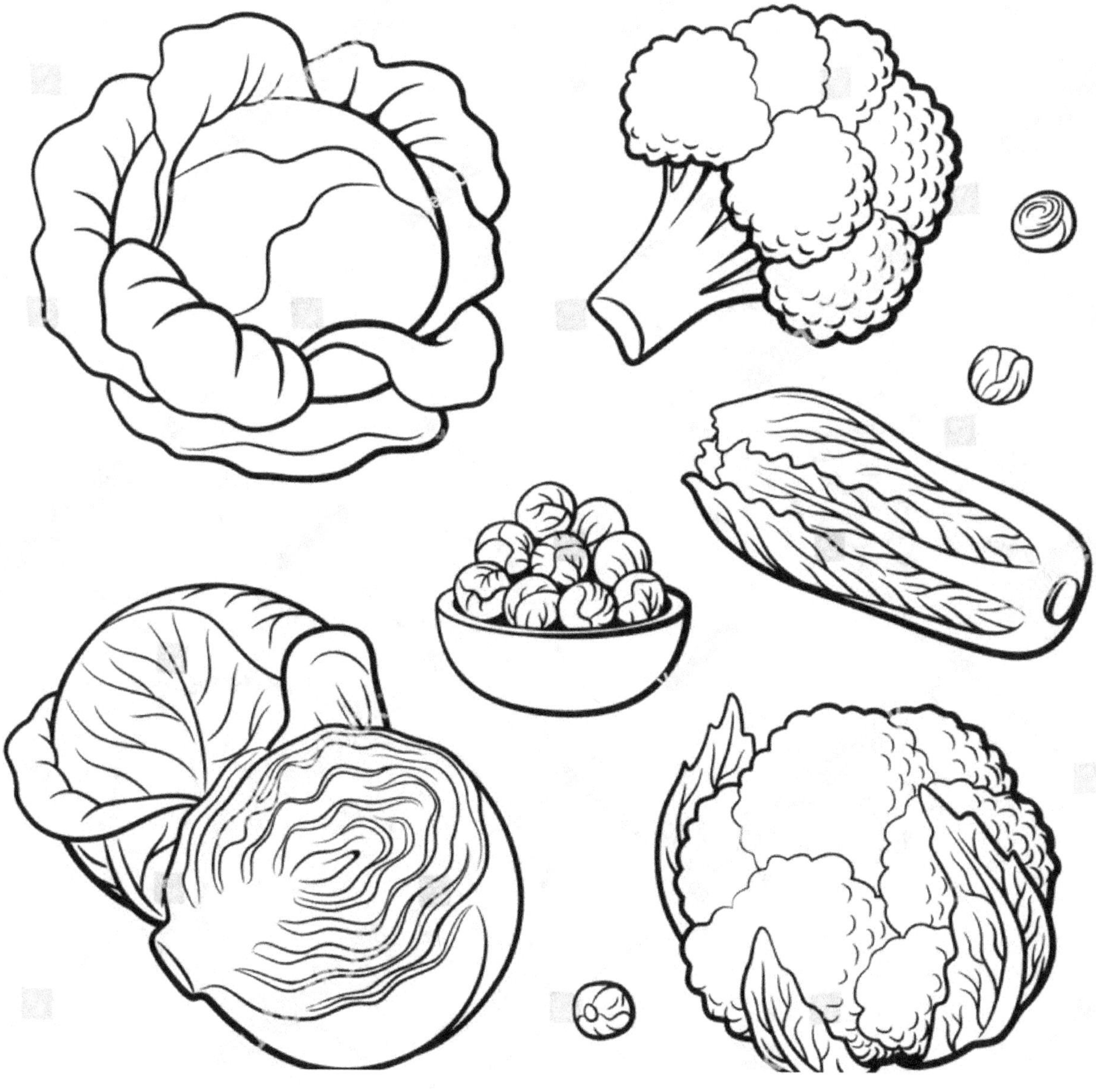

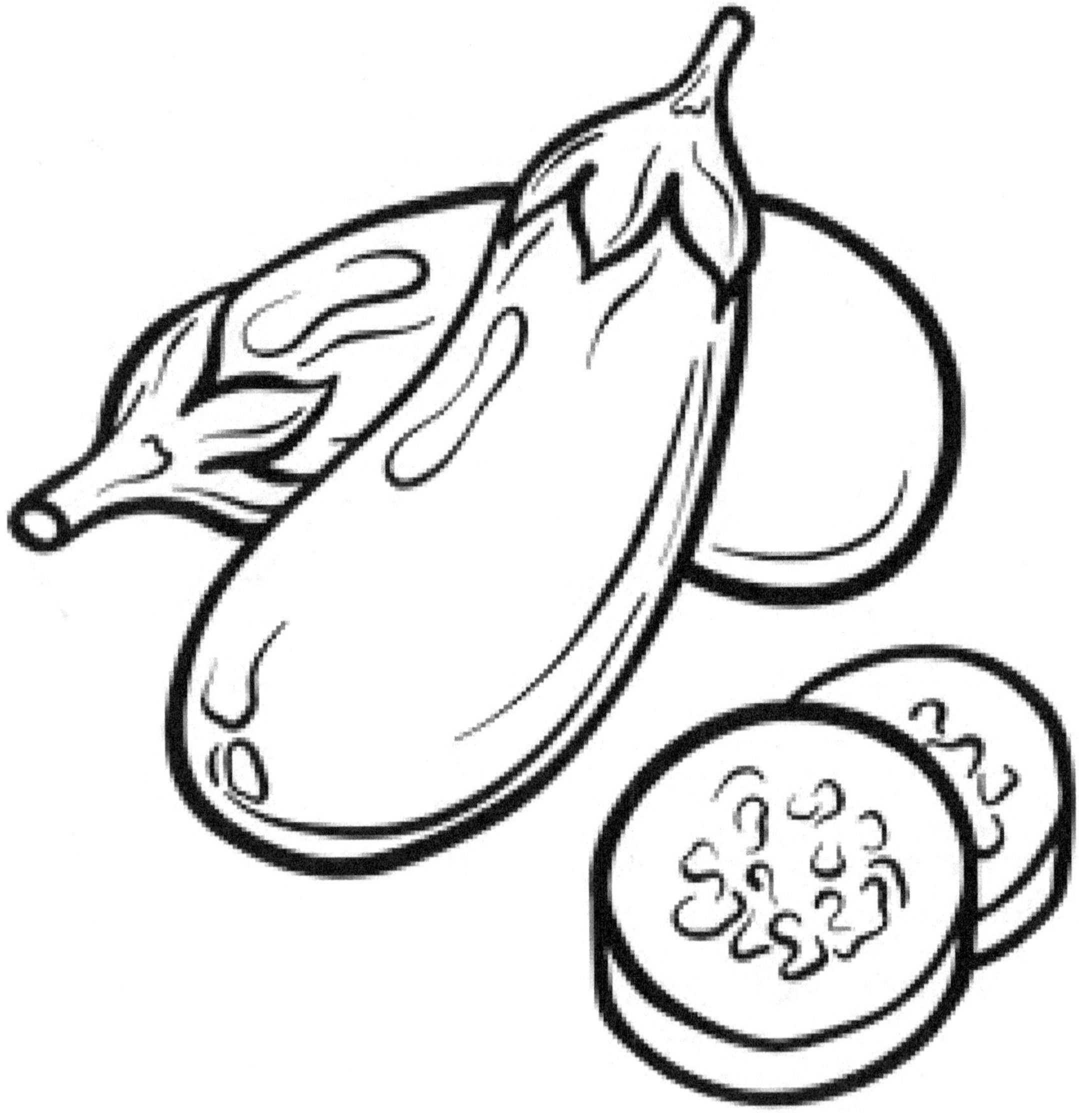

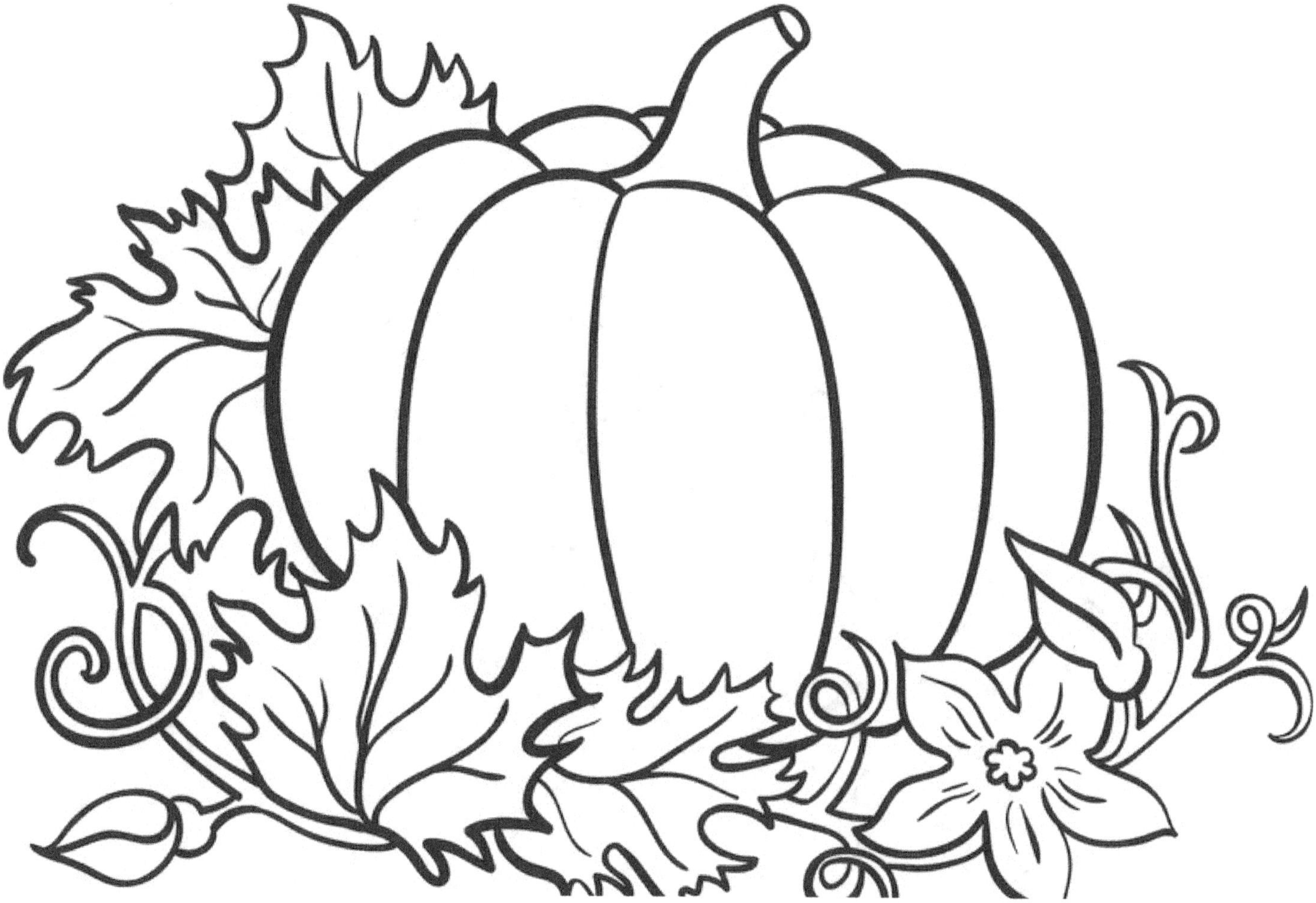

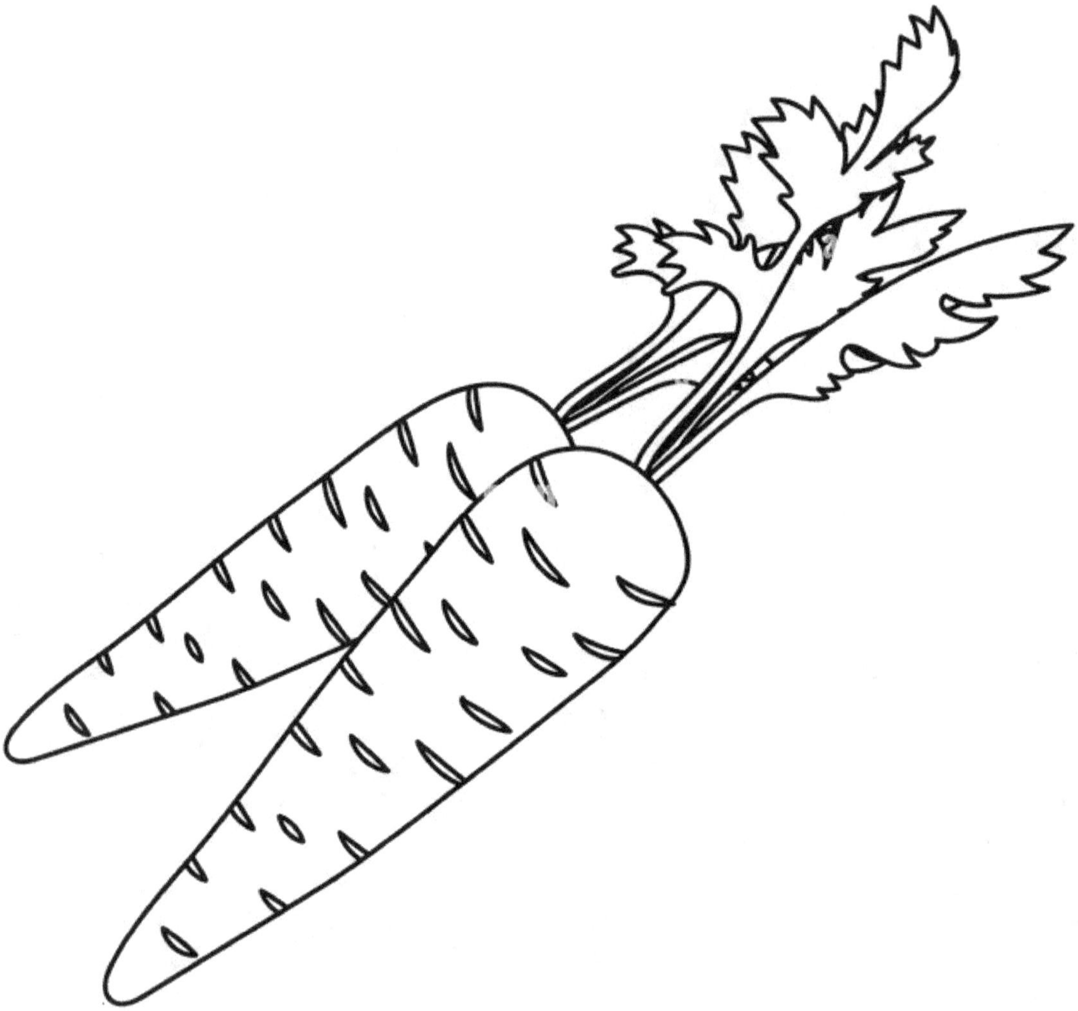

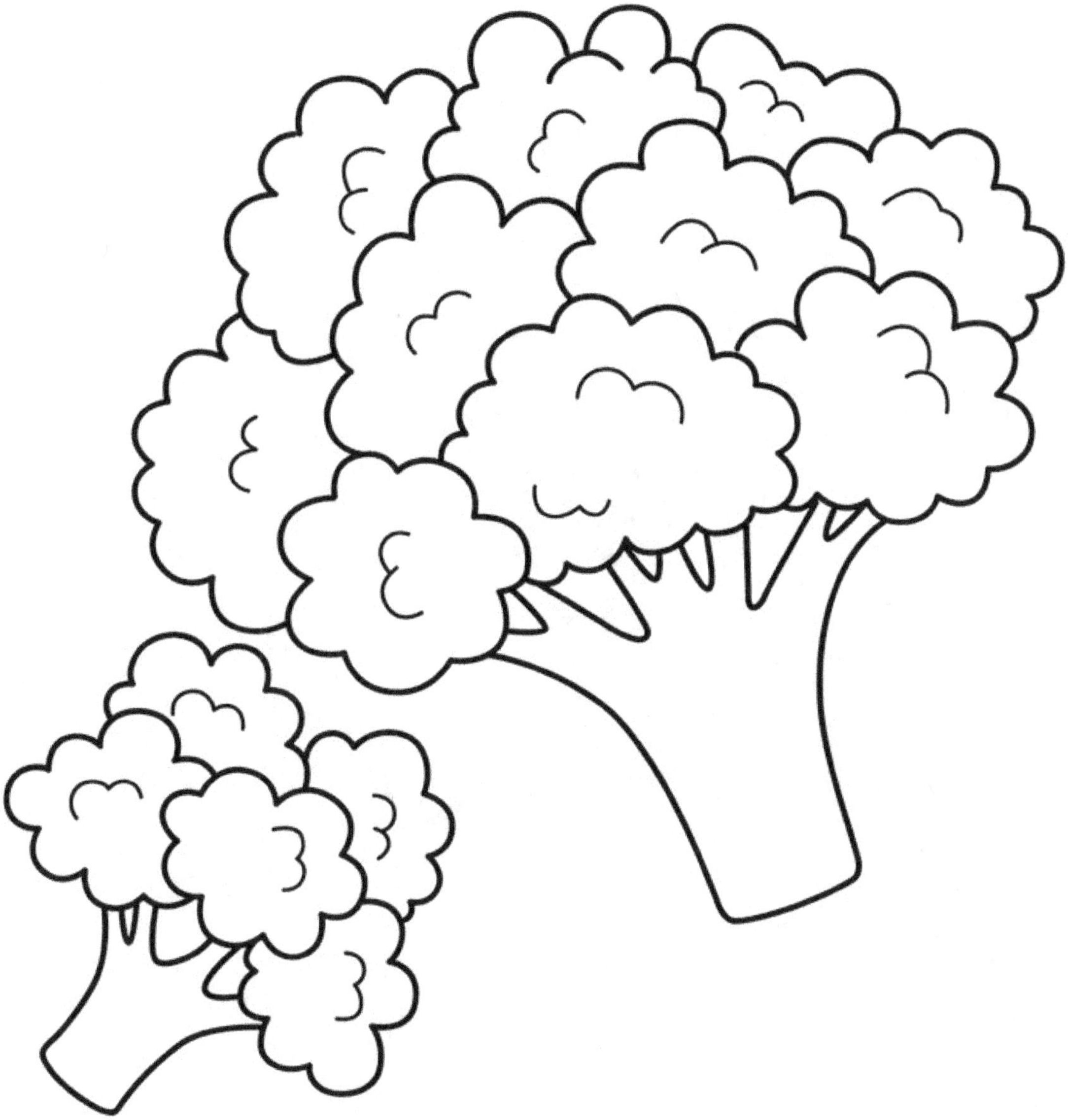

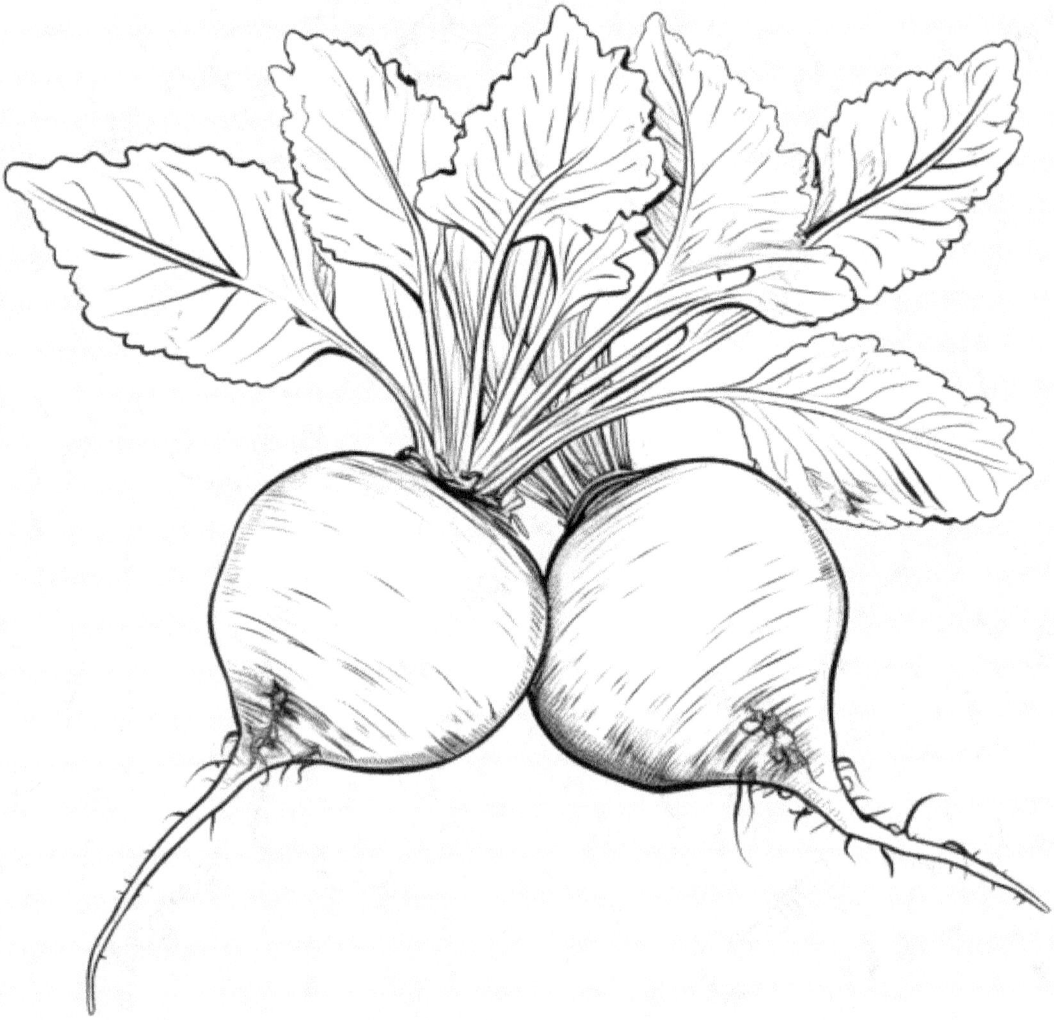

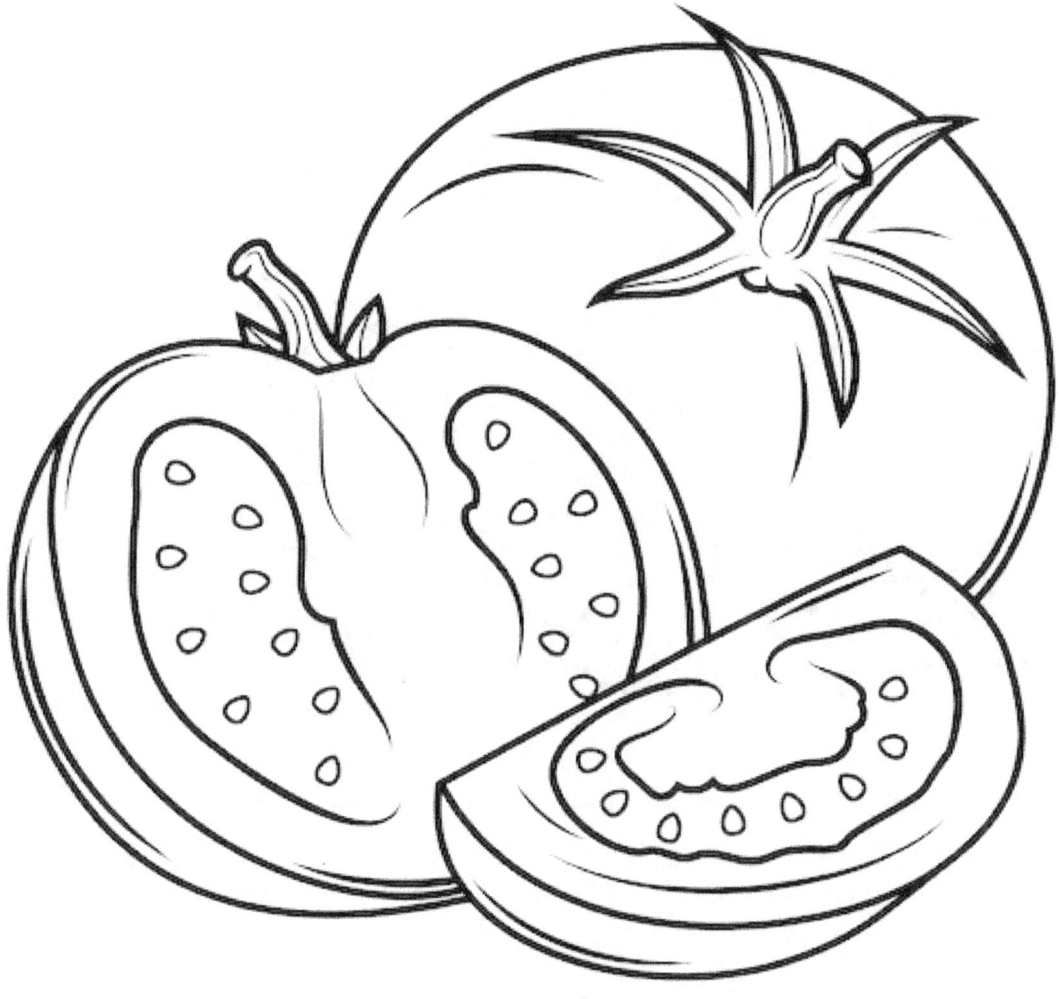

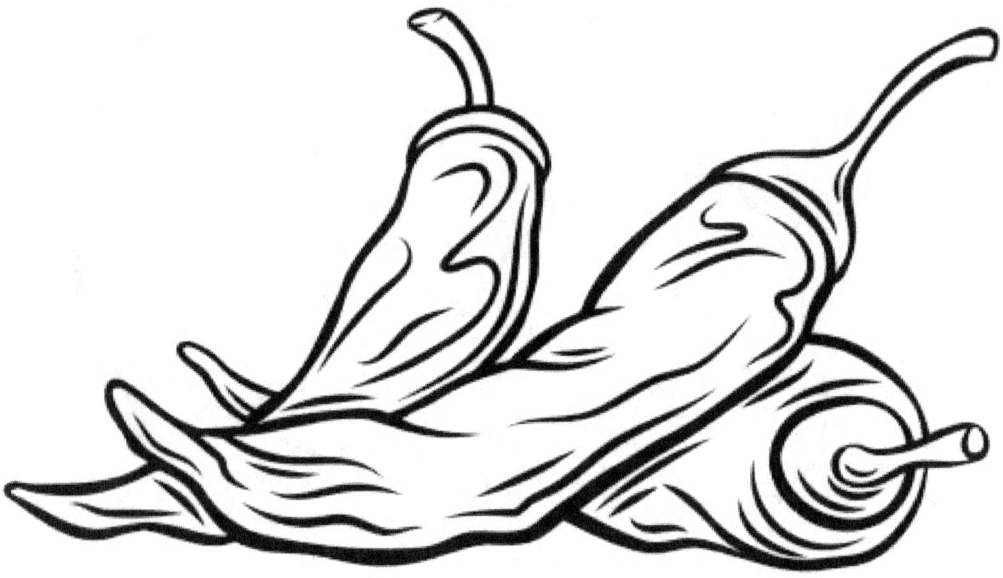

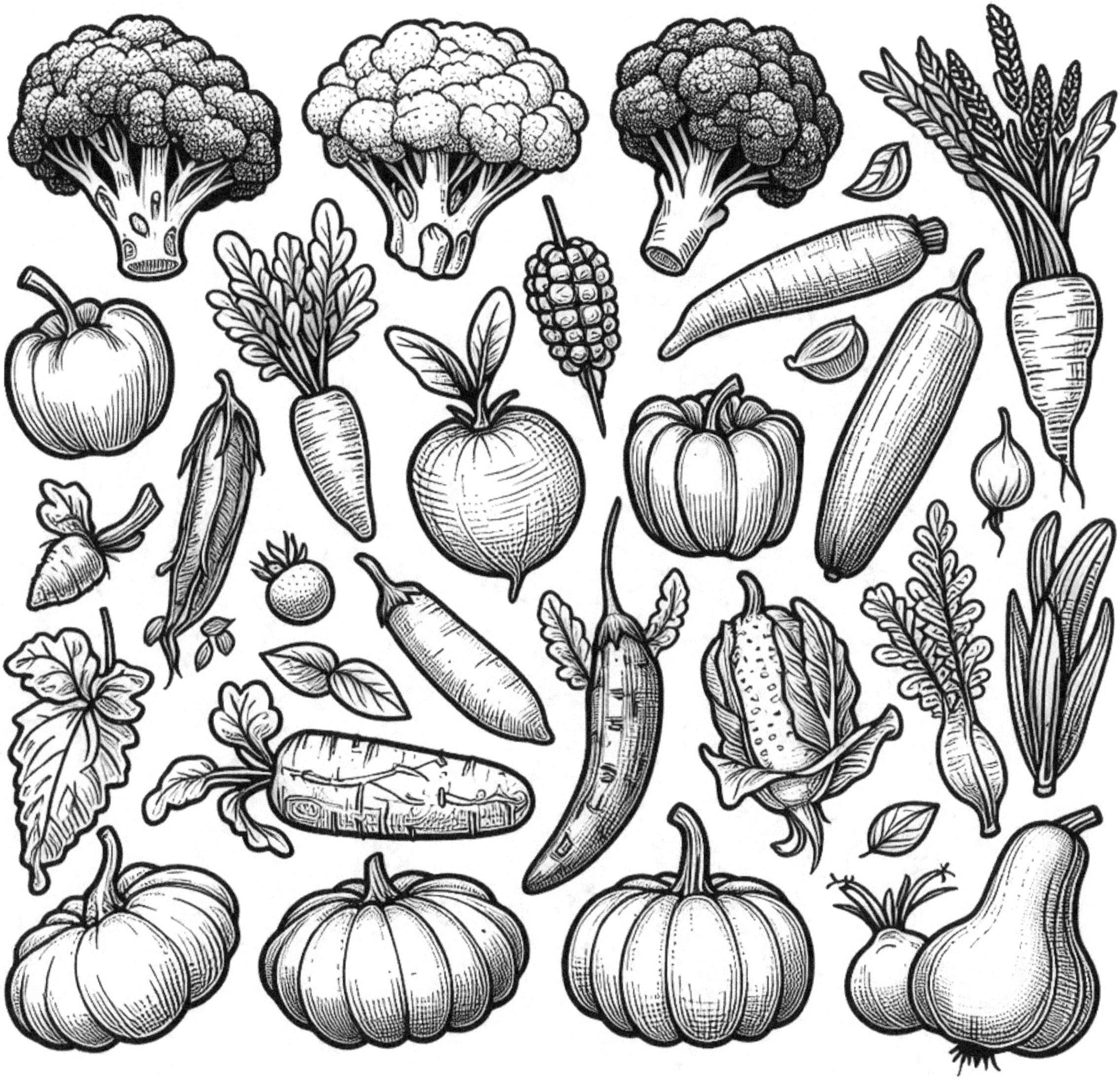

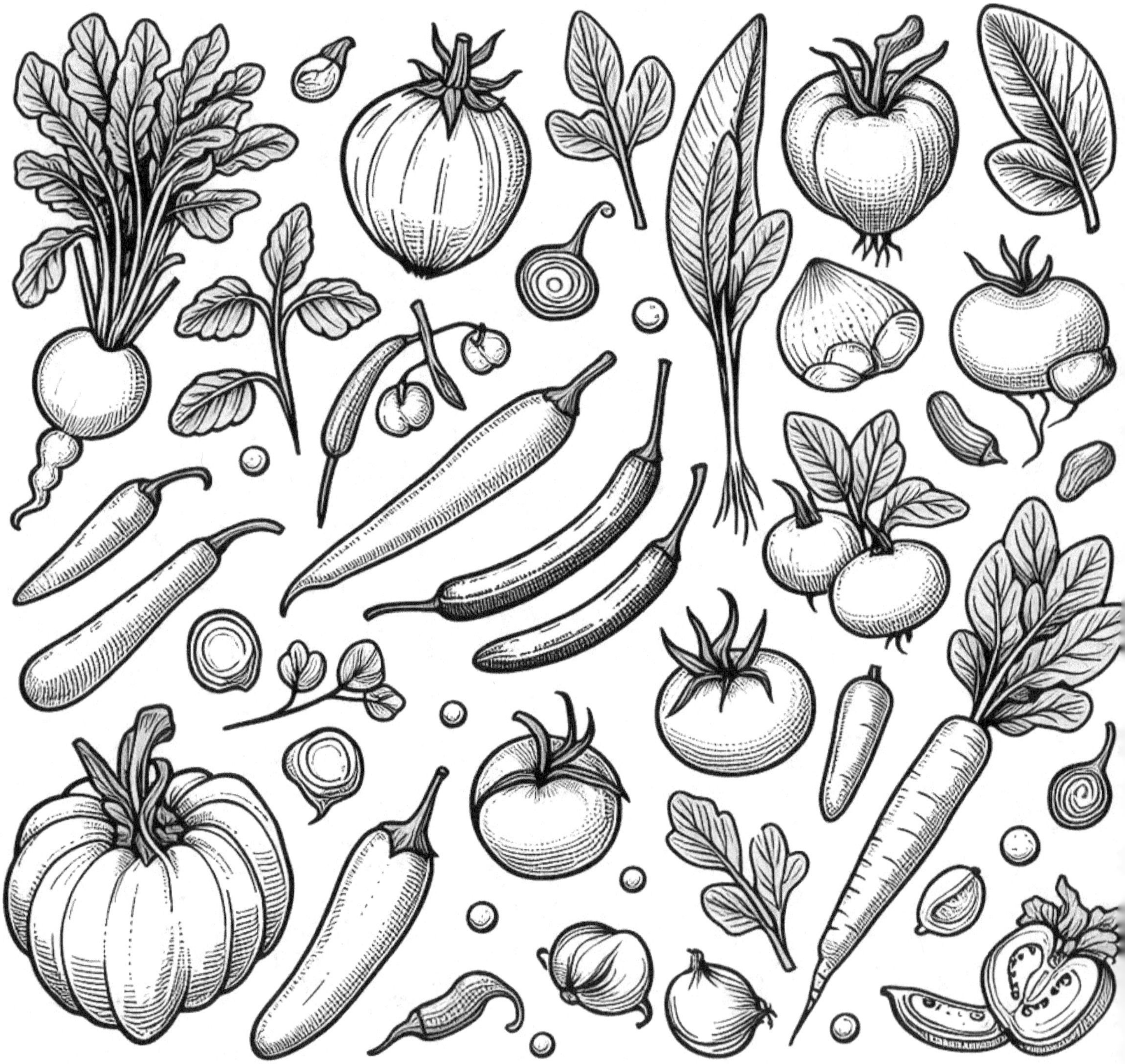

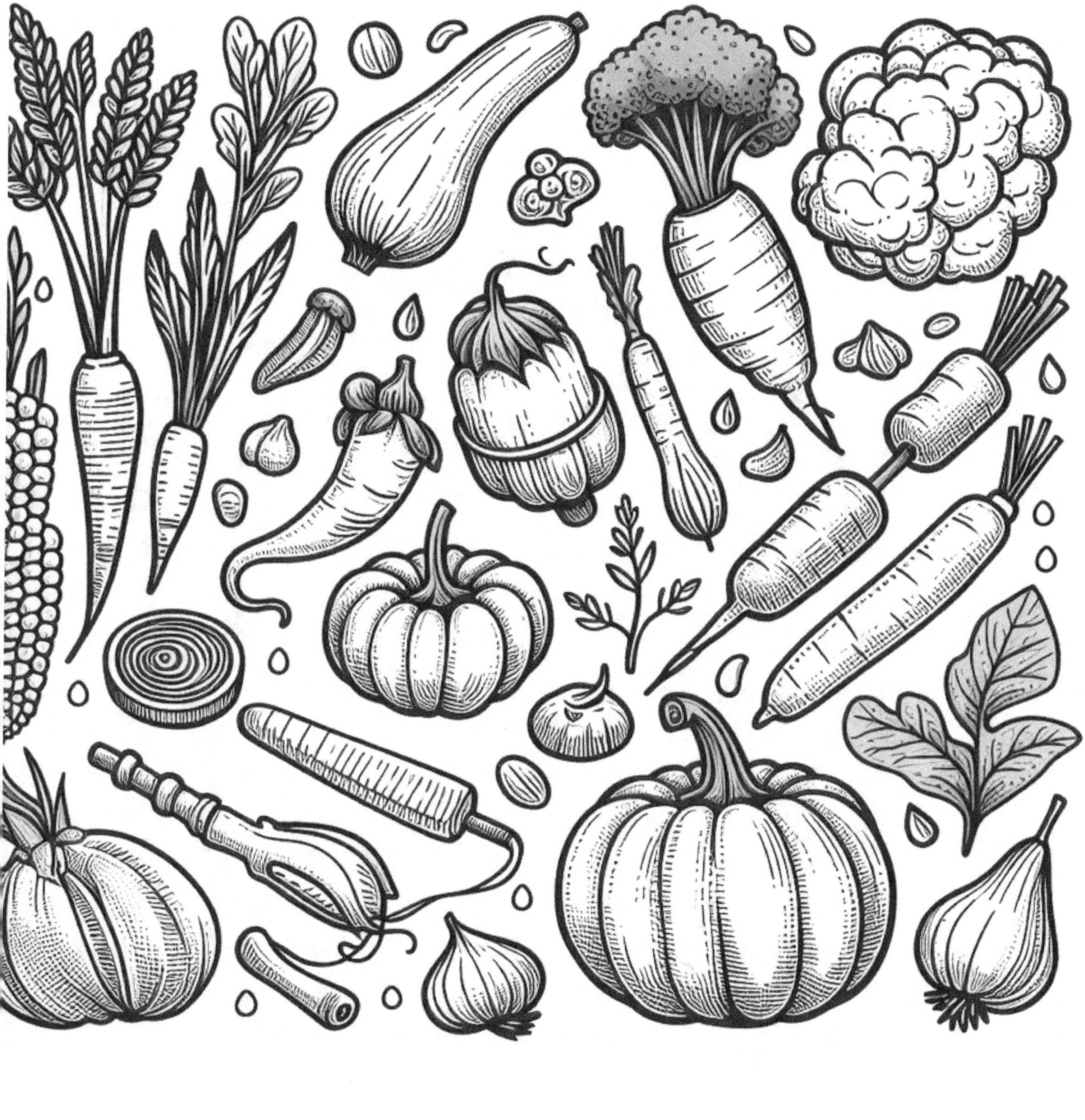

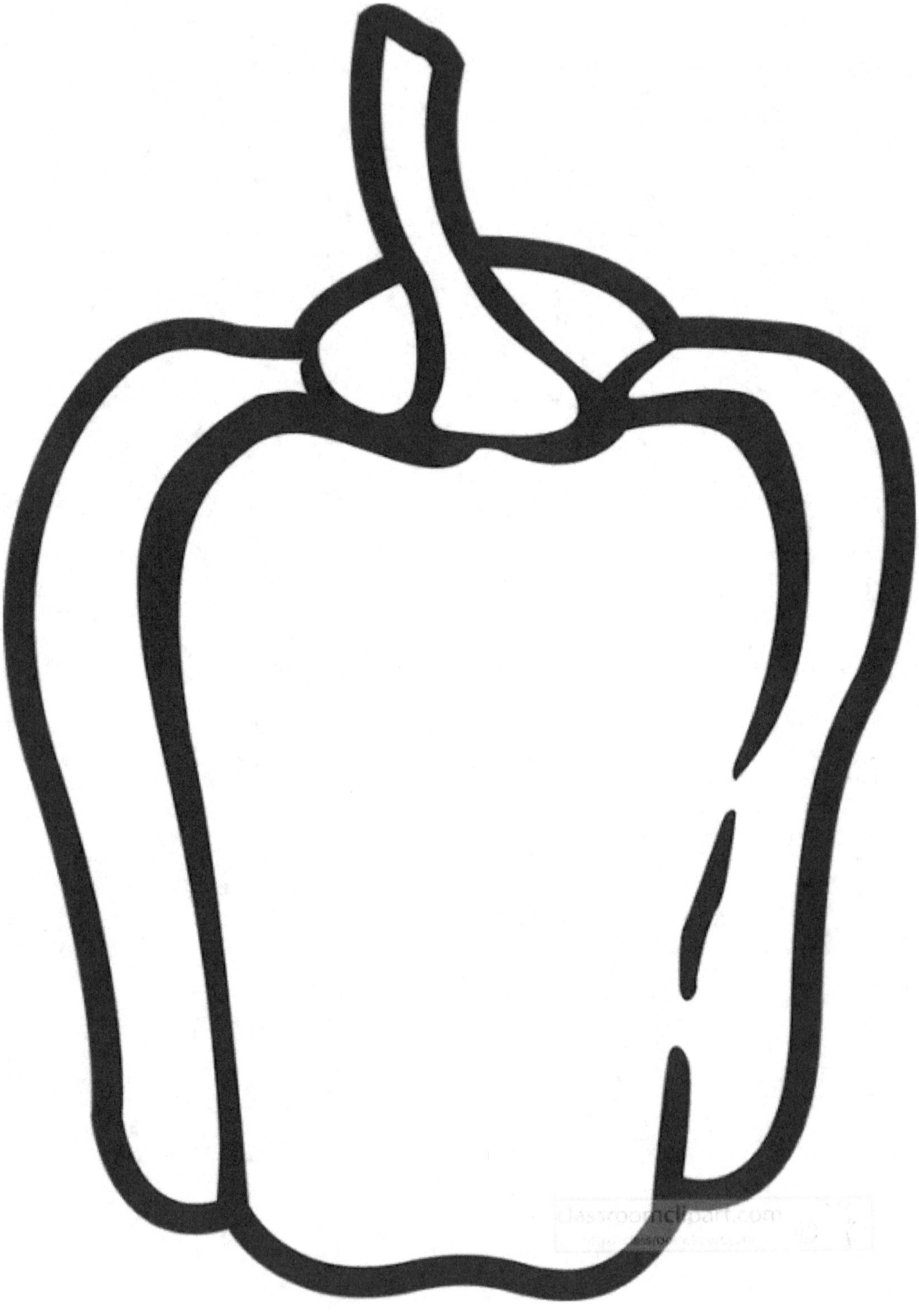
classroomclipart.com

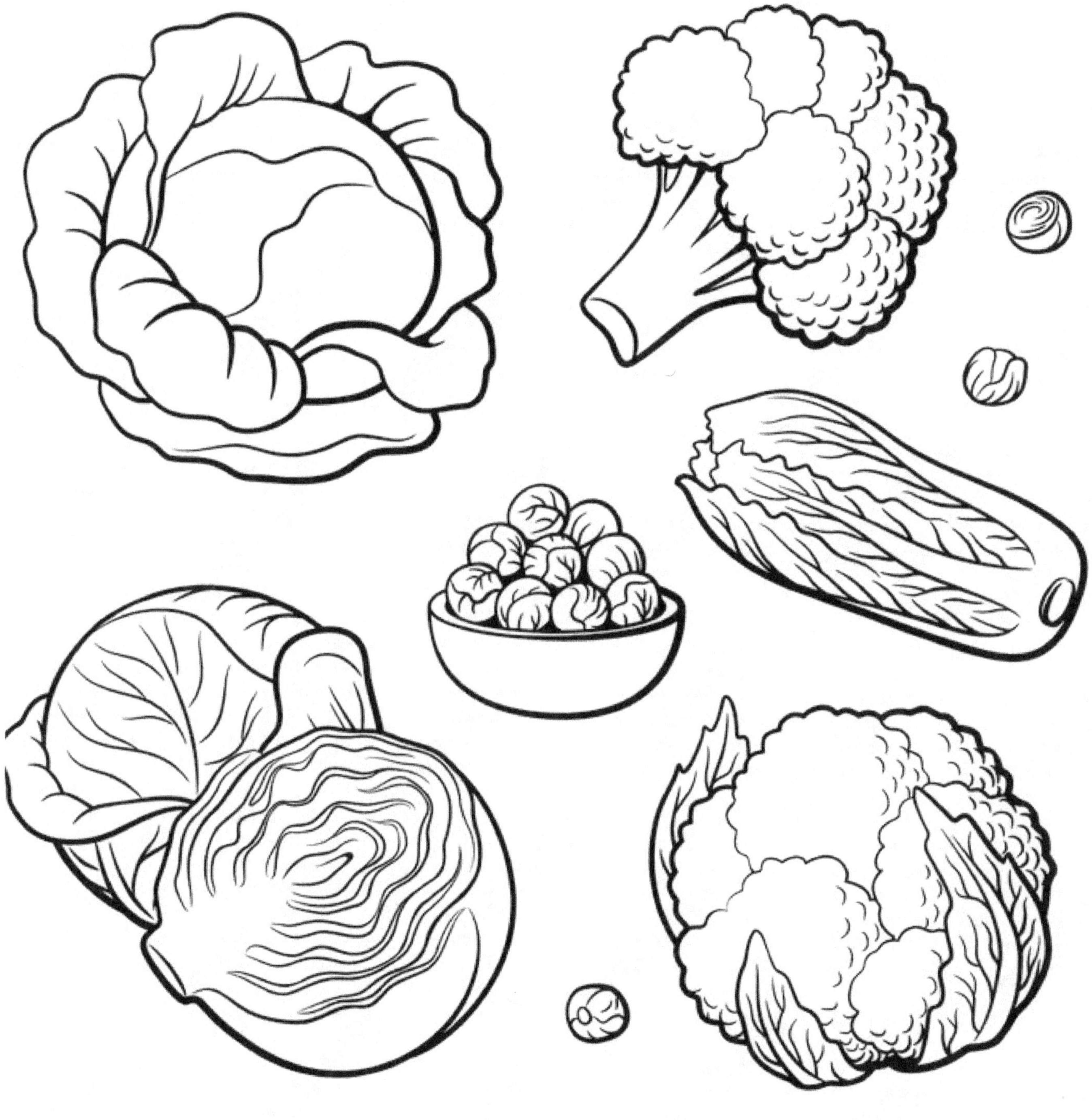

www.ingramcontent.com/pod-product-compliance
Lightning Source LLC
Chambersburg PA
CBHW081022240526
45471CB00018B/3946
9798320034850